LEVEL 3 READER

EVERYTHING AWESOME ABOUT SUPER SHARKS

WRITTEN AND ILLUSTRATED BY

MIKE LOWERY

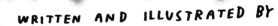

Scholastic Inc.

To Brandon and the Forbeseses
—M.L.

All rights reserved. Published by Scholastic Inc., *Publishers since 1920.* SCHOLASTIC and associated logos are trademarks and/or registered trademarks of Scholastic Inc.

Special thanks to Dr. Christopher Lowe, professor and director of the CSULB Shark Lab, for his guidance and expert verification of the information included in this book.

Photos ©: cover, 1: Alexius Sutandio/Shutterstock; back cover: Makoto Hirose/BluePlanetArchive; 5: Masa Ushioda/BluePlanetArchive; 9: Mark Kostich/iStock/Getty Images; 10: Borut Furlan/WaterFrame/www.agefotostock.com; 13: James D. Morgan/Getty Images; 15: JP Trenque/www.agefotostock.com; 17: Makoto Hirose/BluePlanetArchive; 18: Kelvin Aitken/VWPics via AP Images; 19: Awashima Marine Park/Getty Images; 21: Alexius Sutandio/Shutterstock; 25: Colors and shapes of underwater world/Getty Images; 26: Auscape International Pty Ltd/Alamy Stock Photo; 27: Norbert Probst/imageBROKER/Shutterstock; 29: J. Lambus Photography; 30: Mark Conlin/Alamy Stock Photo.

ISBN 978-1-339-00026-8
10 9 8 7 6 5 4 3 2 1   23 24 25 26 27

Printed in the U.S.A.   40
This edition first printing, 2023
Book design by Doan Buu

TABLE OF CONTENTS

WHAT IS A SHARK?

Most sharks have long bodies and a fin on the end of their tail that they use to propel through the water quickly.

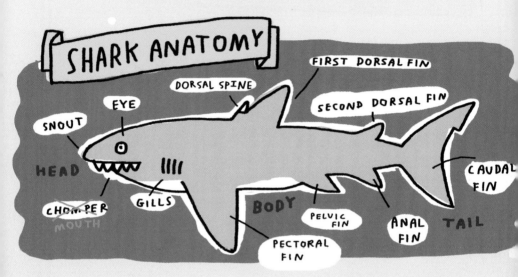

SHARK ANATOMY

FIRST DORSAL FIN
DORSAL SPINE
SECOND DORSAL FIN
EYE
SNOUT
CAUDAL FIN
HEAD
CHOMPER
~~MOUTH~~
GILLS
BODY
PELVIC FIN
ANAL FIN
TAIL
PECTORAL FIN

Most sharks have around 8 fins: **2 dorsal fins, 2 pectoral fins, 2 pelvic fins, 1 anal fin, and a big one for the tail called a caudal fin. These fins help them balance, keep from falling over, speed through the water to catch prey (or if they're late to an appointment), and move in different directions.**

AWESOME FACT!

Sharks don't have typical bones like most fish (or humans). Their skeletons are made out of a rubbery material called cartilage. This is the same bendable stuff that we have in our ears and noses!

MOST SHARKS ARE **MEAT** EATERS, BUT A FEW ALSO EAT PLANTS.

BONNETHEAD SHARK

BONNETHEAD SHARKS ARE KNOWN TO EAT SEAGRASS!

Did you know that not all sharks live in the ocean? Yep! There are sharks that have adapted to live in fresh river water. Like this guy:

NEW GUINEA RIVER SHARK.

THEY CAN GROW UP TO 8 FEET LONG

THEY ARE INCREDIBLY RARE! There may be fewer than 250 alive right now.

THEY HAVE AMAZING SUPERPOWERS!

1. SUPER SKIN!

A shark's skin is actually made of millions of little toothlike bumps called denticles. These denticles help reduce drag when a shark is swimming so it can cut through the water quickly. The denticles even fall out and are replaced—just like teeth!

DENTICLES.

WAIT, DOES THAT MEAN I NEED TO FLOSS... MY SKIN?

2. SUPER SMELL!

Sharks use up to two-thirds of their brain just to process information about SMELL!

3. SUPER EYES!

A shark's eyes have NIGHT VISION, which helps them see in the dark ocean. Sharks' eyes are ten times more sensitive to light than humans' eyes!

Sharks even have an EXTRA EYELID called a nictating membrane. This allows them to see while also protecting their eye.

OPEN   CLOSED

4. SUPER SIXTH SENSE!

Sharks have a special ability to detect ELECTRIC FIELDS in the water! This helps them find prey, such as rays buried in the sand.

5. SUPER TEETH!

Some sharks have MULTIPLE rows of teeth! Some of their teeth are as sharp as knives, and some of them have ridges like a saw blade.

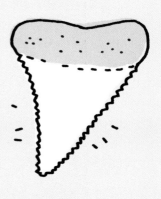

MEGALODON

Lived until 2.6 million years ago.

ITS MOUTH WAS 10 FEET WIDE!

7-INCH-LONG TEETH

Look HOW BIG THEY WERE COMPARED TO A HUMAN!

3 TIMES BIGGER THAN WHALE SHARKS (WHICH ARE THE BIGGEST SHARKS ALIVE TODAY)!

Might have been warm-blooded like white sharks today, which would have made it possible for them to swim in colder water.

Sharks have been around for about 450 MILLION YEARS, which means they're roughly 150 million years older than dinosaurs! They're even older than trees! The megalodon was prehistoric. It is now extinct, which means it no longer exists.

BIGGEST FISH EVER!

#1

ESTIMATED TO HAVE GROWN UP TO **80 FEET LONG!** (THAT'S LONGER THAN A BOWLING LANE!)

ITS NAME ACTUALLY MEANS

GIANT TOOTH!

MEGALODON TOOTH
7 inches

WHITE SHARK TOOTH
Under 3 inches

DANGEROUS SHARKS

TIGER SHARK

WATCH OUT!

DANGER!

Tiger sharks are one of the most dangerous sharks in the world because they eat lots of stuff.

They're like swimming garbage cans! They eat fish, dolphins, jellyfish, birds, squids, and even crocodiles! They've also been known to take bites out of whales!

Shark attacks are pretty rare, but since these guys like to hang out in shallow, warm water, it's possible that they would run into humans.

FOURTH LARGEST SHARK

CAN GROW UP TO 14 FEET LONG!

They typically have around 30 pups per litter, but it's been reported that they can have up to 80!

I'M HUNGRY!

Young tiger sharks have stripes (like a tiger!) but the stripes tend to fade as they get older.

TIGER SHARK

BULL SHARK

WATCH OUT! DANGER!

IT GETS ITS NAME BECAUSE IT'S STRONG LIKE A BULL!

AWESOME FACT!

Most sharks need salt water to survive, but bull sharks have glands near their tails that allow them to store salt when they go into fresh water. They've been spotted hundreds of miles away from the ocean in freshwater rivers!

This is a shark that likes to swim in areas that are warm and shallow...which happens to be where humans like to swim! So sometimes sharks confuse people for prey and attack. Bull sharks actually MIGHT EVEN be the shark species that has attacked the most humans, but we aren't sure. Some scientists think that people misidentify them because their color is similar to other kinds of sharks, leading to incorrect counts of attacks.

JOKE ALERT!

WHY DON'T YOU EAT CLOWN FISH?

THEY TASTE FUNNY!

WHALE SHARK

THE LARGEST LIVING SHARK

(AND THE BIGGEST FISH) IN THE WORLD!

They're filter feeders! They open their mouths really wide to gulp down a bunch of water. They keep the plankton and little fish in their mouths and then spit out the rest.

CAN GROW UP TO 40 FEET LONG!

WOW

HUMAN KID FOR SIZE COMPARISON

They've got more than 3,000 tiny teeth, but they usually just swallow their food whole.

The pattern of spots on their bodies is as unique as our fingerprints. No two whale sharks have the same pattern.

They usually stay close to the surface of the water but are known to dive as deep as 3,200 feet!

NOT RELATED TO WHALES!

They can have up to 300 pups in one litter!

Scientists aren't totally sure how long they can live. Some guess around 60 years, while others estimate that it could be up to 150 years.

WHALE SHARK

BASKING SHARK

CAN FILTER OVER 396,000 GALLONS OF WATER IN AN HOUR! →

CAN GROW UP TO 39 FEET LONG! THAT'S AS BIG AS A BUS!

AWESOME FACT!

Basking sharks are really stinky! Their skin is coated with a slime that helps protect them from parasites, and it can even burn through fishing nets.

BASKING SHARK

They got their name because it looks like they're "basking" (lying in the sun) while they're feeding.

They sometimes jump out of the water, and scientists aren't sure why.

JOKE ALERT!

WHAT'S IN THE OCEAN NEWSPAPER?

CURRENT EVENTS!

SPOOKY SHARKS

GOBLIN SHARK

THIS HAS TO BE ONE OF THE WEIRDEST-LOOKING ANIMALS ON THIS PLANET!

LONG, FLAT SNOUT

SHARP TEETH TO GRAB PREY

Goblin sharks are found in the Atlantic, Indian, and Pacific Oceans. Several have been caught near Japan, where some early fishermen who saw them thought they looked like a Japanese demon called Tengu that has a long, pointed nose. So they called them *tengu-zame* ("zame" means "shark"). Later it was translated to "goblin shark."

AWESOME FACT!

Goblin sharks can jut their jaws out while feeding! Their jaws are attached to elastic ligaments that allow the jaws to move . . . a lot. This very unusual way of biting has been called "slingshot feeding."

GOBLIN SHARK

JOKE ALERT!

WHO IS THE BEST POKER PLAYER IN THE OCEAN?

A CARD SHARK!

SPOOKY SHARKS

FRILLED SHARK

CAN GROW 6 FEET LONG!

Right now you're thinking, "OOPS! That's not a shark, that's an EEL. Right?" Well, I can see why you'd think that! It does look a LOT like an eel ... but it's actually a shark!

FRILLED SHARK

Frilled sharks are considered the most primitive of all shark groups because the ones alive today look a lot like the first sharks from this group to have evolved 150 million years ago.

They aren't seen by humans often because they like to live more than 4,000 feet below the surface. BUT if you did see one, you'd spot right away how it got its name. Its gills aren't split like other sharks' gills and go all the way across the neck, with a red edge!

AWESOME FACT!

Frilled sharks have 25 rows of backward-facing teeth!

It doesn't swim through the water like an eel. It has a HUGE LIVER that is designed to make it able to just hover in the water.

FRILLED SHARK

THAT THING IS REAL?!

DEADLIEST SHARK

WATCH OUT!

WHITE SHARK

DANGER.

Its real name is just white shark, but it's more commonly called great white shark.

(Though they're still not really that deadly to humans!)

Their contracting muscles warm up and allow them to stay warm in cold water.

SOMETIMES → EATS SMALL WHALES!

300 SUPER-SHARP TEETH →

Can grow up to 19–21 feet long and weigh over 4,000 pounds!

CAN SWIM UP TO 20 MPH!

IT WAS AN ACCIDENT!

NOT A BAD GUY!

Though the white shark is one of the sharks most responsible for human injury, and even death, they're still not very dangerous to humans. Sharks aren't interested in eating us, and a bite is usually just because the shark is curious or a little confused. To a shark, a swimmer in the ocean might look like a strange object or a tasty seal!

A shark doesn't have hands like we do. It may examine an unfamiliar object with its mouth, which could result in injury to a human. Divers have also been bitten while harassing sharks, which means the shark was simply defending itself.

In 2022, there were only 5 deaths as the result of shark attacks.

WHITE SHARK

AWESOME FACT!

THEY CAN ROLL THEIR EYES!

WHAT-EV-ERRR!

White sharks don't have nictitating membranes (those protective extra eyelids) like some sharks do, so they have another way of protecting their eyes. If they sense danger, they can roll their eyes back into their skull!

SHARK VACATION!

TIME FOR A BREAK!

From April to July, white sharks meet in a spot in the middle of the ocean between Hawaii and Mexico. For years scientists weren't sure why they chose this location, but recently they noticed some males were diving to catch animals that live deep in the ocean. This is why it's often called "The White Shark Café."

TOTALLY GROSS SHARK
GREENLAND SHARK

Greenland sharks are scavengers! They've been known to eat live seals as well as dead animals, like reindeer and even polar bears!

It was first captured on film in 1995, and it was 18 years before anyone got them on video again.

TOTALLY GROSS!

Ommatokoita elongata

MOST GREENLAND SHARKS ARE BLIND BECAUSE OF A 2-INCH-LONG PARASITE THAT **LIKES TO STICK** TO **THEIR EYES!**

Some scientists think they can live to be up to

400 YEARS OLD

or even older.

WE MADE IT!

That means that some of the Greenland sharks alive today might have been born before the *Mayflower* landed at Plymouth Rock!

One of the largest sharks in the world, it grows up to 21 feet long and can weigh 2,100 pounds!

AWESOME FACT!

The Greenland shark's flesh is really poisonous! It contains enzymes that protect the sharks against cold water and high pressure, and those enzymes are toxic for humans.

THEY SWIM REAAAAAALLY SLOWWLLY.

They typically swim less than 1 mile an hour... but that's still faster than slugs move!

(Slugs only go around .19 miles per hour!)

WHOA! HE'S SO FAST!

AWESOME-LOOKING SHARKS

HAMMERHEAD SHARK!

Can grow up to 14 feet long!

Eats fish, small sharks, rays, octopuses, and squids.

There are at least 10 species of hammerheads, and 3 are endangered.

DOESN'T LAY EGGS LIKE MOST FISH, INSTEAD IT GIVES BIRTH TO LIVE YOUNG.

AWESOME FACT!

The hammerhead shark has sensors on its head that pick up electrical signals of its prey!

Its oddly shaped head gave it its name, but it's also designed to help increase *lift*, like how an airplane's wings help it stay in the air. It also helps with rapid turning!

IMMUNE TO RAY VENOM.

Has to move its head to the side to look forward.

Having eyes on the end of its head allows it to scan quickly for food.

HAMMERHEAD SHARK

SAWSHARK

THEY EAT OTHER SHARKS AND EVEN CROCODILES!

AWESOME FACT!

Sawsharks use their strange snouts to stun their prey by whacking them!

33,

THEY HAVE 2 LONG BARBELS to HELP THEM FIND FOOD ON THE OCEAN FLOOR.

CAN GROW UP TO 5 FEET LONG.

THEY GET CAUGHT EASILY IN FISHING NETS, AND THEY'RE CURRENTLY ENDANGERED.

SAWSHARK

SAWLIKE SNOUT, LINED WITH TEETH! (IT'S CALLED A ROSTRUM.)

TASSELED WOBBEGONG SHARK

Those things sticking out that look like tree branches are actually barbels! These sharks have bad eyesight and use their barbels to help feel around for prey.

Wobbegong sharks aren't dangerous to humans, unless a human accidentally steps on one!

THEIR NAME MEANS "SHAGGY BEARD."

I CAN ONLY GROW A MUSTACHE.

CAN GROW UP TO 4 FEET LONG.

AWESOME FACT!

Wobbegong sharks don't actively hunt. They lie in wait for prey to get close enough, and then they SNAP really quickly to catch them with their strong jaws and sharp teeth.

WOBBEGONG SHARK

COOKIECUTTER SHARK

aka cigar shark

Up to 22 inches long.

SUPER WEIRD!

Can dive as deep as 3,200 feet.

They've even caused trouble for submarines! A cookiecutter shark took bites out of some rubber that was on a sub's sonar device... and it made the crew unable to see where they were going!

Their bottom teeth fall out all at once, and then the shark swallows the teeth!

Why the strange name? They use their sharp teeth to take quick bites out of their prey before they swim off.

First it uses its lips to stick to prey like a suction cup, then it spins its body and uses its teeth to carve out a chunk 2 inches across and 2.5 inches deep! They like to bite animals that are a lot bigger than them, like whales, dolphins, seals, tuna, swordfish, marlin, and even white sharks!

COOKIECUTTER SHARK

AWESOME FACT!

ITS BELLY CAN GLOW!

It might do this to blend in with moonlight and trick prey swimming below. Cookiecutter sharks can even keep glowing after they die—up to 3 HOURS!

EVEN MORE SHARKS!

SWELL SHARK

To scare off predators, they're able to pump water into their bodies and "swell" up to twice their size! They can also do this with air when they're at the surface of the water, and they even BURP out the air when the danger is gone!

BUURRP!

If a swell shark inflates itself between rocks, it's tougher for a predator to pull it out.

SWELL SHARK

NURSE SHARK

THEY SUCK UP THEIR FOOD LIKE A VACUUM!

It can swim really fast, but only for short bits of time.

Not aggressive. It sleeps all day on the floor of the ocean and swims around at night looking for food.

PACIFIC ANGEL SHARK

They've got a flat body, with their mouth in the front like a ray. They also have long, needlelike teeth. Their eyes are on the top of their head and so are spiracles, which they use like a snorkel to suck in clean water when they're lying in mud. They're usually about 5 feet long, and they've got simple barbels.

I'M NOT A RAY! I'M A SHARK!

PEOPLE OFTEN ACCIDENTALLY MISIDENTIFY THEM AS RAYS.

spiracles

They live on the ocean floor near kelp forests and rocky reef.

HIDE-AND-SEEK CHAMPS!

They're an ambush predator...which means they like to hide and wait for prey to swim by. They have special muscles that pump water over their gills so they don't need to keep swimming like other sharks to get oxygen.

MAKO SHARK

THEY CAN JUMP 15 FEET OUT OF WATER

LONG, POINTY TEETH LIKE DAGGERS!

CAN SWIM UP TO 30 MPH!

SAVE THE SHARKS

If you've been following along, you've learned that sharks are pretty dangerous, but only to other fish and the creatures they eat in the ocean. They're not very dangerous to humans. Attacks do happen, but they're rare and typically only occur when the sharks are provoked or when it's a case of mistaken identity.

When it comes to sharks versus people, sharks are actually the ones that are in danger. They have been overfished and hunted for so long they could even go extinct! Some sharks that are currently threatened include white sharks, mako sharks, basking sharks, whale sharks, and many others. And sharks aren't the only sea creatures in trouble.

THE OCEANS AND THE CREATURES THAT LIVE IN THEM ARE SUPER AWESOME, BUT THEY NEED OUR HELP!

It's estimated that by **2050** the ocean will contain more plastic than fish. But we can change things! You can help by recycling, avoiding single-use plastics, and volunteering for beach cleanups.